ANIMAL JOKES

Compiled by Pam Rosenberg • Illustrated by Mernie Gallagher-Cole

Published by The Child's World®
1980 Lookout Drive
Mankato, MN 56003-1705
800-599-READ
www.childsworld.com

The Child's World®: Mary Berendes, Publishing Director
Editorial Directions, Inc.: E. Russell Primm, Editorial
Director; Lucia Raatma, Copyeditor and Proofreader;
Jennifer Zeiger and Joshua Gregory, Editorial Assistants
The Design Lab: Design and production

Library of Congress Cataloging-in-Publication Data
Animal jokes / compiled by Pam Rosenberg ;
illustrated by Mernie Gallagher-Cole.
    p. cm.
  ISBN 978-1-60253-515-2 (library bound : alk. paper)
  1. Animals—Juvenile humor. I. Rosenberg, Pam.
II. Gallagher-Cole, Mernie. III. Title.
  PN6231.A5A55   2010
  818'.602080362—dc22   2010002046

Printed in the United States of America
Mankato, Minnesota
June 2011
PA02099

ABOUT THE AUTHOR

Pam Rosenberg is the author of more than 50 books for children. She lives near Chicago, Illinois, with her husband and two children.

ABOUT THE ILLUSTRATOR

Mernie Gallagher-Cole lives in Pennsylvania with her husband and two children. She has illustrated many books for The Child's World®.

TABLE
OF
CONTENTS

MARINE AND FISH JOKES

Q: Which side of a fish has the most scales?
A: The outside.

....

Q: What do you get from a bad-tempered shark?
A: As far away as possible.

....

Q: What do you call a fish with no eyes?
A: Fsh.

....

Q: What kind of gum do whales chew?
A: Blubber gum.

....

Q: What is the best way to talk to a fish?
A: Drop it a line.

Q: Who held the
baby octopus
for ransom?
A: Squid-nappers.

Q: Why are goldfish orange?
A: The water makes them rusty.

Q: Why is a fish easy to weigh?
A: Because it has its own scales.

Q: What's the difference between a fish and
a piano?
A: You can't tuna fish.

Q: Why are fish so smart?
A: They spend a lot of time in schools.

COW JOKES

Q: What newspaper do cows read?
A: The *Daily Moos*.

Q: What do you call a sleeping cow?
A: A bull-dozer.

JAMIE: Why is the barn so noisy?
OSCAR: Because all the cows have horns.

Q: How did the rancher count his cows?
A: With a cow-culator.

Q: What goes, "Boo, boo, boo"?
A: A cow with a cold.

DANIEL: How can you tell if a bull is about to charge?
ANNA: He takes out his credit card.

Q: What do cows get when they are sick?
A: Hay fever.

FARM JOKES

FARMER: Did you realize that it takes three sheep to make one sweater?
CITY SLICKER: Really? I didn't even know they could knit!

Q: What kinds of horses frighten ranchers?
A: Night-mares.

Q: What did the farmer say when he wanted to get the sheep's attention?

A: "Hey, ewe!"

Q: Why did the baby turkey stuff down its food?

A: Because he was a little gobbler.

Q: What do you get if you cross a sheep with a kangaroo?

A: A woolly jumper.

WILD ANIMAL JOKES

Q: What do you call a bear with no ears?

A: B.

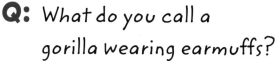

Q: What do you call a gorilla wearing earmuffs?

A: Anything you like. It can't hear you!

Q: What kind of bear goes out in the rain?

A: A drizzly bear.

Q: What do you get when you cross a porcupine with a balloon?

A: POP!

Q: How does a hedgehog play leapfrog?

A: Very carefully.

Q: What's worse than an alligator with a toothache?

A: A centipede with athlete's foot.

INSECT JOKES

Q: What kind of ant is good at math?
A: An Account-ant.

Q: Why did the elephant put his trunk across the path?
A: To trip up the ants.

Q: What did the clean dog say to the insect?
A: "Long time, no flea."

Q: What game does an elephant play with an ant?

A: Squash.

Q: Why did the moth eat a hole in the carpet?

A: Because he wanted to see the floor show.

Q: What does the caterpillar do on New Year's Day?

A: It turns over a new leaf.

Q: What do you get if you cross a flea and a rabbit?

A: Bugs Bunny.

Q: What did one firefly say to the other?

A: "Got to glow now!"

Q: What's the difference between a bird and a fly?

A: A bird can fly, but a fly can't bird.

Q: What did one flea say to the other after a night out?

A: "Shall we walk home or take a dog?"

Q: What is the biggest ant in the world?

A: An eleph-ant.

Q: What do you call a bee that can't make up its mind?

A: A may-bee.

Q: Why do bees hum?

A: Because they forgot the words.

Q: What goes zzub, zzub?

A: A bee flying backward.

Q: What do you call a crate full of ducks?
A: A box of quackers.

Q: When is the best time to buy canaries?
A: When they are going cheap.

Q: What kind of math do owls like the most?
A: Owl-gebra.

Q: Which bird is always out of breath?
A: A puffin.

13

Q: What do you get when you cross a woodpecker with a carrier pigeon?

A: A bird that knocks before delivering its message.

Q: What do you get if you cross a parrot with a centipede?

A: A great walkie-talkie.

CAT
JOKES

Q: What happened when the cat swallowed a ball of wool?

A: It had mittens.

Q: Why did the cat want to use the computer?
A: Because it saw the mouse.

Q: What do you call it when a cat bites?
A: Catnip.

Q: What do you get if you cross a cat with a bottle of vinegar?
A: A sourpuss.

Q: Why was the cat so small?
A: Because it only drank condensed milk.

Q: Why do cats make terrible storytellers?
A: They only have one tail.

Q: What did the cat do when he swallowed some cheese?
A: He waited by the mouse hole with baited breath.

MOUSE JOKES

Q: What has six eyes but cannot see?
A: Three blind mice.

Q: What is gray and squirts jam at you?
A: A mouse eating a doughnut.

CHICKEN JOKES

Q: Why does a chicken coop have two doors?
A: Because if it had four doors, it would be a sedan.

Q: What do you get if you cross a centipede with a chicken?
A: Enough drumsticks to feed an army.

Q: Why did the rooster run away?
A: Because it was a chicken.

Q: What do you call it when a bunch of chickens play hide-and-seek?
A: Fowl play.

DOG JOKES

Q: What kind of dog does Dracula have?
A: A bloodhound.

KATIE: I lost my dog.

MATT: Why don't you put an ad in the paper?

KATIE: What good would that do? My dog can't read.

Q: Why is a dog so warm in the summer?
A: It wears a coat and pants.

Q: What happened when the dog went to the flea circus?
A: He stole the show.

Q: What flower do dogs like best?
A: A collie-flower.

Q: When does a dog go, "Moo"?
A: When it's learning a new language.

Q: When is a dog most impolite?
A: When it points.

Q: What did the dog say when he sat on sandpaper?
A: "Ruff!"

Q: Why do skunks like to argue?
A: Because they like to raise a stink.

SARAH: Where are you taking that skunk?

JAKE: To the gym.

SARAH: What about the smell?

JAKE: Oh, he'll get used to it.

Q: What do you get when you cross a fish with an elephant?

A: Swimming trunks.

Q: What's big and gray with horns?

A: An elephant marching band.

Q: What's as big as an elephant but weighs nothing?

A: An elephant's shadow.

Q: What do you give an elephant with big feet?

A: Plenty of room.

Q: What do you get if you cross an elephant and a kangaroo?

A: Big holes all over Australia.

Q: Why is the elephant braver than the hen?

A: The elephant isn't a chicken.

FROG JOKES

Q: When is a car like a frog?
A: When it's being toad.

Q: Where do frogs keep their money?
A: In a river-bank.

Q: What did the frog dress up as for Halloween?
A: A prince.

Q: What do frogs like to drink in the winter?
A: Hot croako.

Q: What happens when two frogs run into each other?

A: They get tongue-tied.

Q: What's green and slimy and found at the North Pole?

A: A lost frog.

Q: What do stylish frogs wear?

A: Jump-suits.

BIG CAT JOKES

Q: What is striped and bouncy?

A: A tiger on a pogo stick.

Q: What happened when the lion ate the comedian?

A: He felt funny.

Q: What do you get if you cross a tiger with a sheep?

A: A striped sweater.

....

Q: What do you call a show full of lions?

A: The mane event.

....

Q: How does a leopard change its spots?

A: When it gets tired of one spot, it just moves to another.

....

Q: What happened to the farmer who tried to cross a lion with his goat?

A: He had to get a new goat.

....

Q: What do you get when you cross a tiger with a watchdog?

A: A terrified mailman.

....

Q: What is the fiercest flower in the garden?

A: A tiger lily.